How to

Make

Fascinators

Dr Miriam Kinai

Contents

1

What Is A Fascinator?

Fascinators are stylish head decorations which can be worn instead of hats.

Fascinators can be worn as evening accessories in which case they are called cocktail hats, or in weddings as bridal hair accessories instead of a veil or as stylish millinery by fashionista guests.

These statement making hair accessories can also be worn for Church services, funerals, trendy parties as well as fashionable social events such as the Concours d'Elegance, Royal Ascot, Grand National and the Melbourne Cup.

Fascinators can be classified as:

1. Feather fascinators

2. Flower fascinators

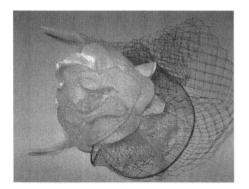

3. Cocktail hat fascinators

4. Beaded fascinators

4. Bridal fascinators

Some fascinators can fit in several categories simultaneously.

Dr Miriam Kinai

2

How To Make Cone Base Fascinators

Millinery Supplies

Scissors

Multipurpose glue

Needle with dark thread

6" x 6" or 15cm x 15cm card to make the base

6" x 6" or 15cm x 15cm black or dark colored piece of fabric to cover the base exterior

3" x 3" or 7.5cm x 7.5cm black or dark colored piece of fabric to cover the base interior

Fabric flowers, netting, lace, ribbons, beads, rhinestones or feathers to decorate your fascinator

Clips to attach the fascinator to your hair

Instructions

1. Draw a circle in the card with a 5" or 12cm diameter. Cut it out.

2. Cut a straight line from the edge of the circle to its center.

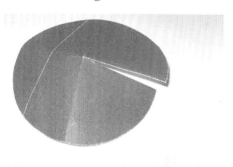

3. Overlap 1" or 2.5 cm of the cut edges to create a cone shape and glue them in place.

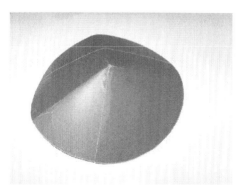

4. Glue the large piece of dark fabric to the top of the cone base.

5. Glue the overhanging fabric edges to the inside of the cone.

6. Glue the small piece of dark fabric to the inside of the cone to cover the raw edges.

7. Place the decorative elements of your fascinator on the outside of your cone in the following layers:

The first or bottom layer with the "background" netting, lace and large feathers.

The second or middle layer with the "statement" fabric flower or feathery plume.

The third of top layer with the "filler" ribbons, rhinestones, beads and small feathers.

Try out different layouts and reposition them until they are esthetically pleasing to your eyes. Once you are satisfied, glue or sew them in place. Note that you do not have to use all these layers.

6. Attach the clip to the inside of your cone either by gluing it or sewing it.

✴✴✴✴✴

3

How To Make A
Side Comb Fascinator

Millinery Supplies

Scissors

Multipurpose glue

Needle with dark thread

Side comb

Ribbon

Fabric flowers, netting, lace, ribbons, beads, rhinestones or feathers to decorate your fascinator

Instructions

1. Glue one end of your ribbon to the side comb end and wrap the ribbon around the comb going between the comb's teeth. When you get to the other edge of the comb, glue the ribbon end firmly in place.

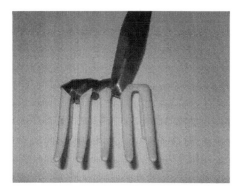

2. Place the decorative elements of your fascinator on the ribbon covered side comb in the following layers:

The first or bottom layer with the "background" netting, lace and large feathers.

The second or middle layer with the "statement" fabric flower or feathery plume.

The third of top layer with the "filler" ribbons, rhinestones, beads and small feathers.

Try out different layouts and reposition them until they are esthetically pleasing to your eyes. Once you are satisfied, glue or sew them in place. Note that you do not have to use all these layers.

✶✶✶✶✶

4

How To Make A Headband Fascinator

Millinery Supplies

Multipurpose glue

Needle with dark thread

Headband

Fabric flowers, netting, lace, ribbons, beads, rhinestones or feathers to decorate your fascinator

Instructions

1. Glue one end of your ribbon to the headband and wrap the ribbon around the headband. When you get to the other edge of the headband, glue the ribbon end firmly in place.

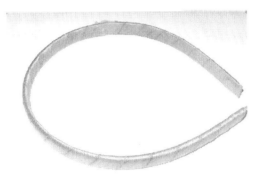

2. Place the decorative elements of your fascinator on the ribbon covered head band in the following layers:

The first or bottom layer with the "background" netting, lace and large feathers.

The second or middle layer with the "statement" fabric flower or feathery plume.

The third of top layer with the "filler" ribbons, rhinestones, beads and small feathers.

Try out different layouts and reposition them until they are esthetically pleasing to your eyes. Once you are satisfied, glue or sew them in place. Note that you do not have to use all these layers.

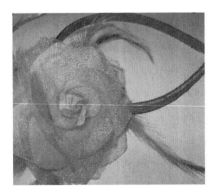

✸✸✸✸✸

About The Author

Dr. Miriam Kinai is an integrative medical doctor.

You can visit her blog at
http://www.TheBestSellingEbooks.blogspot.com/

or follow her on twitter at http://twitter.com/AlmasiHealth

Email enquiries to drkinai@yahoo.com with BOOKS as your subject.

Books By Dr Miriam Kinai
Natural Body Products Series

These books teach you how to make skincare products as well as the benefits of various vegetable oils, essential oils, butters, and herbs to help you choose the best ingredients. These books contain recipes for normal, sensitive, mature, and dry skin as well as for managing cellulite, eczema, psoriasis, menopause, PMS, painful periods, arthritis, stress, sadness, mental fatigue, and insomnia. Books in this series include:

1. How to Make Handmade Natural Bath Bombs

2. How to Make Handmade Natural Bath Melts

3. How to Make Handmade Natural Bath Salts

4. How to Make Handmade Natural Bath Teas

5. How to Make Handmade Natural Body Butters

6. How to Make Handmade Natural Body Lotions

7. How to Make Handmade Natural Body Scrubs

8. How to Make Handmade Natural Healing Balms

9. How to Make Handmade Natural Herb Infused Oils

10. How to Make Handmade Natural Soap

11. How to Make Natural Skincare Products - this book teaches you how to make bath bombs, bath melts, bath salts, bath teas, body butters, body lotions, body scrubs, healing balms, herbs, and soaps.

Aromatherapy Essential Oils Guide

Aromatherapy Essential Oils Guide teaches you the characteristics, health benefits, and uses of the following commonly used essential oils:

Chamomile (Roman) essential oil, Clary sage essential oil, Eucalyptus essential oil, Geranium essential oil, Lavender essential oil, Lemon essential oil, Peppermint essential oil, Rosemary essential oil, Tea tree essential oil, Ylang ylang essential oil.

*****

Aromatherapy Carrier Oils Guide

Aromatherapy Carrier Oils Guide teaches you how to dilute aromatherapy essential oils with carrier or base oils and explains the characteristics and uses of the following commonly used carrier oils:

Sweet almond oil, Sunflower oil, Olive oil, Jojoba, Evening primrose oil, Virgin Coconut oil, Fractionated Coconut oil, Apricot kernel oil, Avocado oil, Rose hip oil.

It also teaches you how to dilute essential oils with carrier oils.

*****

How to Blend Essential Oils

How to Blend Essential Oils teaches you how to mix aromatherapy oils so that you can create healing mixtures with pleasant scents.

These therapeutic blends can then be used to create healing massage oils, handmade lotions, homemade soap and hand poured scented candles.

*****

How to Plan a Cheap, Chic Wedding

How to Plan a Chic, Cheap Wedding teaches you step by step wedding planning so that you can know how to plan a beautiful wedding even if you are on a tight budget.

Table of Contents

Chapter 1. The Pre-Wedding Activities

These are the activities you should be engaging in once you decide that you want to get married regardless of whether or not you are dating.

Chapter 2. The Key Events of any Wedding Planning Timeline

Understanding the key factors in any wedding timeline will enable you to plan weddings with a full year's notice or with just a month's notice without missing any important detail.

Chapter 3. The Chief Categories of Costs in any Wedding Plan

Our wedding planning checklist will help you understand the key cost categories of all weddings so that you can successfully plan weddings of all sizes from large social events to small intimate gatherings.

Chapter 4. How to Fit a Wedding into any Budget

Knowing how to fit a wedding into any budget will make you a more successful wedding planner as you will be able to cater to brides in different social groups as well as be able to adjust your wedding plans when the bride and groom encounter unexpected financial hitches.

Chapter 5. Free Resources

Knowing where to get free wedding resources such as software, wedding music and templates on the web will help you plan wonderful weddings.

Managing Stress with the Word of God

Managing Stress with the Word of God teaches you how to manage stress effectively by combining time tested Biblical principles with medical proven relaxation techniques.

Topics covered in this book include:

1. What is stress?

2. What is the body's response to stress?

3. Symptoms of Stress

4. Biblical Principles for Stress Management

5. Medical Relaxation Techniques

6. Other Stress Relief Activities

*****

Rules Of Relaxation

Rules of Relaxation teaches you 130 simple relaxation techniques as it covers the A to Z of stress management from Assert yourself, Breathe deeply, Cast your burdens, Drink herbal teas, Establish social support, Formulate realistic goals, Guard your heart, Have complementary hobbies, Identify personal stressors, Jaunt, Keep the Sabbath, Listen to music, Meditate on the Word, Nab a nap, Optimize stress, Pamper yourself, Quash sin, Reason rationally, Schedule news fasts, Trust God, Use cognitive restructuring, Veto worry, Work out, eXperiment with aromatherapy, Yield to God to Zap job stress.

*****

Sword Words

SWORD WORDS teaches you how to wage Christian spiritual warfare using the SWORD of the Spirit which is the WORD of God. (Ephesians 6:17)

It instructs you how to wield your SWORD WORDS together with the full armor of God. It demystifies the enemy's devices and explains the battle plan. It also tells you how to position yourself strategically and communicate effectively with your backup so that you can win your battles regardless of whether you are fighting for your marriage, children, or finances or fighting addictions, opposition, and fear.

Resolving Conflicts just like Jesus Christ

Resolving Conflicts just like Jesus Christ uses Biblical examples from Jesus Christ to King Solomon to teach Conflict Resolution Strategies, Third Party Mediation Techniques, Conflict Reduction and Prevention so that you can increase the peace in your home, the productivity of your ministry, and the profitability of your business.

Christian Anger Management

Christian Anger Management teaches Biblical anger management tips and self help strategies to help you manage anger instead of letting it manage you and destroy your testimony, life, family, and career.

Managing Stress For Teens

Managing Stress for Teens teaches teenagers Biblical principles, medical techniques, and life skills to manage 80 common teenage stressors.

It teaches them how to resist using alcohol, cigarettes, drugs, and how to overcome addiction. It edifies them to resist sexual temptation, fornication, pornography, homosexuality, and lesbianism. It also helps them cope with sickness, and disability.

Managing Stress for Teens also teaches teenagers how to manage emotions such as anger, anxiety, confusion, fear, guilt, loneliness, love, lust, low self confidence, and shyness. It guides them on how to deal with negative peer pressure. It also trains them to cope with family problems like abuse.

Managing Stress for Teens suggests constructive activities for teens who don't have money. It helps also helps them understand parental issues like pressure from parents and schools them on the best way to deal with bullying.

Managing Stress for Teens also clarifies issues on God, Jesus, The Holy Spirit, feeling they lack faith, and living right. It coaches them on how to deal with fashion trends, crime, corruption, and cultural practices. It also helps them understand puberty, their body shape, self image, gender realization and the effects of negative thoughts and words as well as helping them answer the questions "Who am I?" and "Why am I here?"

Dark Skin Dermatology Color Atlas

Dark Skin Dermatology Color Atlas is filled with clear explanations and color photos of skin, hair, and nail diseases affecting people with skin of color or Fitzpatrick skin types IV, V, and VI.

Topics covered include Acne Vulgaris, Alopecia Areata, Anal Warts, Angioedema, Aphthous Ulcers, Atopic Dermatitis, Blastomycosis, Blister Beetle Dermatitis or Nairobi Fly Dermatitis, Cellulitis, Chronic Ulcers, Confetti Hypopigmentation, Cutaneous T Cell Lymphoma, Cutaneous Tuberculosis, Dermatitis Artefacta, Erythema Nodosum, Exfoliative Erythroderma, Gianotti Crosti Syndrome, Hand Dermatitis , Hemangioma, Herpes Zoster, Ichthyosis, Ingrown Toenails, Irritant Contact Dermatitis, Kaposi Sarcoma, Keloids, Keratoderma Blenorrhagica, Klippel Trenaunay Weber Syndrome, Leishmaniasis, Leprosy, Leukonychia, Lichen Nitidus, Lichen Planus, Lichenoid Drug Eruption, Linear Epidermal Nevus, Linear IgA Dermatosis (LAD), Lipodermatosclerosis, Lymphangioma Circumscriptum, Miliaria, Molluscum Contagiosum, Neurofibromatosis, Nickel Dermatitis, Onychomadesis, Onychomycosis, Palmoplantar Eccrine Hidradenitis, Papular Pruritic Eruption (PPE), Paronychia, Pellagra, Pemphigus Foliaceous, Pemphigus Vulgaris, Piebaldism, Pityriasis Rosea, Pityriasis Rubra Pilaris, Plantar Hyperkeratosis, Plantar Warts, Poikiloderma, Postinflammatory Hyperpigmentation and Hypopigmentation, Post Topical Steroids Hypopigmentation, Psoriasis, Pyogenic Granuloma or Lobular Capillary Hemangioma, Scabies, Seborrheic Dermatitis, Steven Johnson Syndrome (SJS) and Toxic Epidermal Necrolysis (TEN), Sunburn, Systemic Sclerosis, Tinea Capitis, Tinea Pedis, Tinea Versicolor, Traction Alopecia, Urticaria, Vasculitis, Vitiligo, and Xanthelasma.

Made in the USA
Lexington, KY
01 October 2012